LIFE-SAVING TOOLS

Learning to draw Superman and his friends is a fun, easy adventure. Follow the instructions carefully, and soon you'll be creating super action scenes all by yourself!

LET'S GET STARTED! FIRST, YOU'LL NEED SOME TOOLS.

PENCILS

Pencil leads range from soft to hard—B, HB, F, and H. Try them all, and then pick the ones you like best.

MARKERS

Gather a large assortment of colored markers. Choose fat-tipped ones and some with small points. You'll also need a few black markers to finish your drawings.

PAPER

There are all kinds of paper. Smooth, white paper is best for comic book drawings.

ERASERS

You may need lots and lots and lots of them! Don't worry if you make mistakes—everyone does, including professional artists. (Keep this to yourself, but cartoonists go through more erasers than pencils!)

COLORED PENCILS

Soft leads work best. Your drawings will come to life if you use markers and colored pencils together!

STRAIGHTEDGE

A straightedge is handy for drawing buildings and backgrounds. A triangle, ruler, or anything that makes a straight line will do.

ARE YOU READY? YOU'RE GOING TO START WITH SOMETHING INCREDIBLY EASY... SCRIBBLING!

CURVES

Relax! The most important lines for drawing are strong, smooth curves, so practice drawing them on scraps of paper. Use your whole arm when you draw, and get used to how it feels to draw from your shoulder, rather than your hand and wrist.

CIRCLES

Keeping a loose, relaxed grip, sketch circles of all sizes around your paper. Be light and quick about it!

No marks for neatness here—you have permission to scribble. You're just getting warmed up.

CLARK'S TIPS

YECHH!

DON'T make little scratchy lines when you draw. Be bold! Make each circle with one smooth line.

OVALS

Now draw ovals and egg shapes.

Keep the shapes loose and light. Make them small, large, fat, or thin.

Remember, good drawing comes from using your whole arm, not just your hand and wrist. See if you can do that.

STARTED 3-D

3-D DRAWINGS

You've been exercising your arm—now it's time to exercise your brain! Take those ovals and circles you've drawn, and imagine them as 3-D objects!

CYLINDERS

If you connect two identical ovals with straight lines, you create a tube or cylinder.

Tubes are not always long and thin. They can be tall, short, fat, or skinny. Check out how many objects around you are made of tube shapes.

YOU'RE DOING GREAT! KEEP THAT 3-D THINKING GOING, AND WE'LL PUT IT ALL TOGETHER IN ONE PAGE!

BOXES

Boxes are just as easy! Join squares and diamonds of the same size with parallel lines.

Many things are made of box shapes—cars, guns, houses, etc.

Look for simple shapes in the things around you.

PROPORTIONS III

THIS IS THE ONLY PART OF THE BOOK THAT'S EVEN SLIGHTLY TOUGH—PROMISE! BUT YOU CAN DO IT!

A

B

1

C

D

2

Make sure to leave a little space here!

3

4

Proportion is the correct size of things in relation to other things. To get the figure in the right proportion, start with a stick figure skeleton. Draw a vertical line and divide it into four equal sections. Draw lightly—the lines won't be part of your finished drawing, but they help to guide you. Divide the top half into four more sections.

Draw the spine. It should run from section A to halfway through section D. For the ribs, draw an egg shape that fits inside sections B and C, leaving a smidgen of space at the top and bottom. Make these spaces exactly like they are above. Draw a watermelon shape resting on the bottom of section D for the hips.

Add an egg shape for the head, which fits inside section A. (Your figure will be 8 heads high.) Draw the legs straight down from the outside of the hips to the ground. Bet you already noticed that the knees are exactly halfway between the hips and the ground!

How big is the head compared with the ribs? The shoulders compared with the head?

Copy these stick figures carefully.

These are called gesture drawings because they establish action and movement.

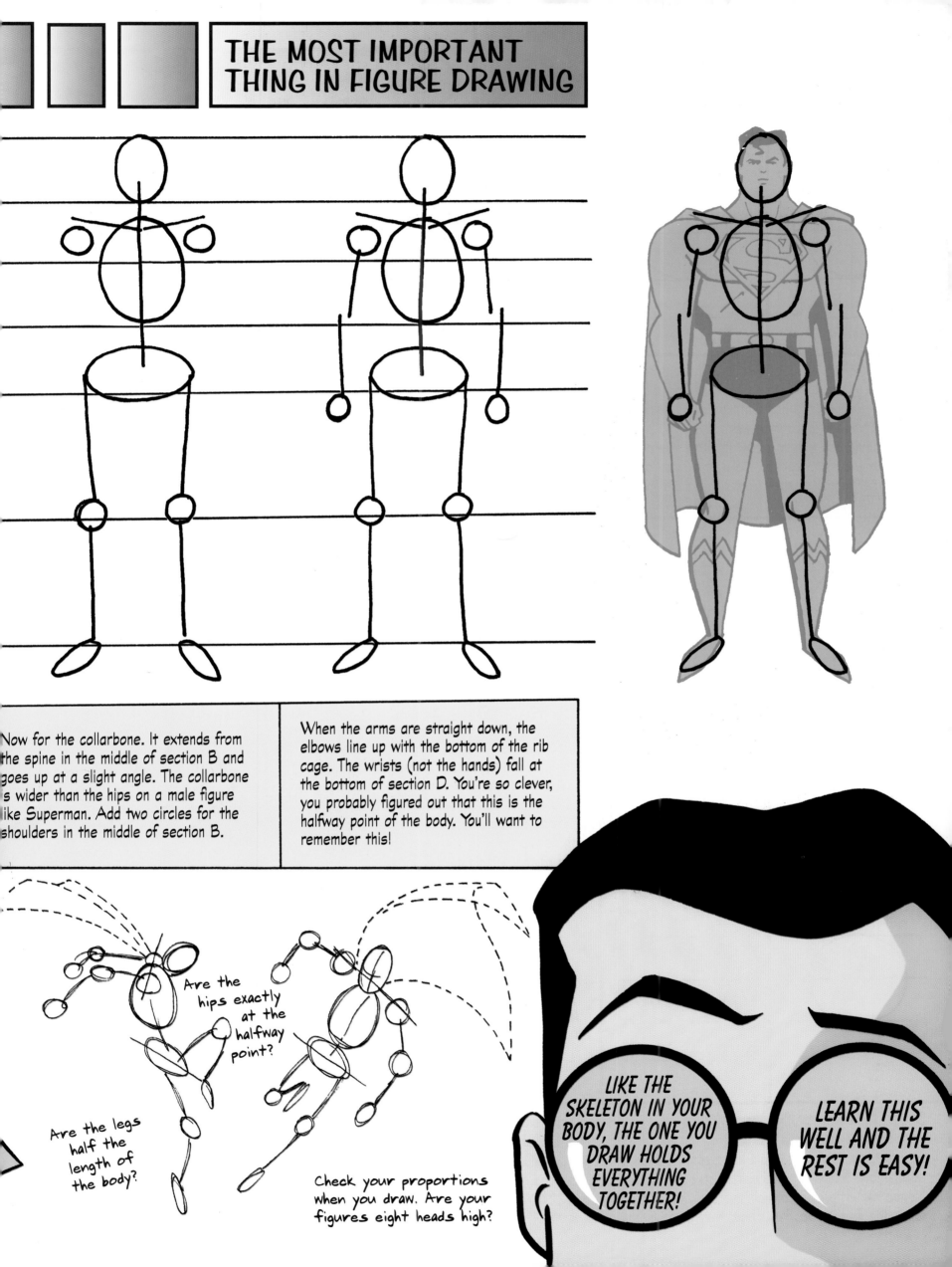

THE MOST IMPORTANT THING IN FIGURE DRAWING

Now for the collarbone. It extends from the spine in the middle of section B and goes up at a slight angle. The collarbone is wider than the hips on a male figure like Superman. Add two circles for the shoulders in the middle of section B.

When the arms are straight down, the elbows line up with the bottom of the rib cage. The wrists (not the hands) fall at the bottom of section D. You're so clever, you probably figured out that this is the halfway point of the body. You'll want to remember this!

Are the hips exactly at the halfway point?

Are the legs half the length of the body?

Check your proportions when you draw. Are your figures eight heads high?

LIKE THE SKELETON IN YOUR BODY, THE ONE YOU DRAW HOLDS EVERYTHING TOGETHER!

LEARN THIS WELL AND THE REST IS EASY!

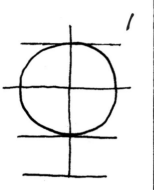  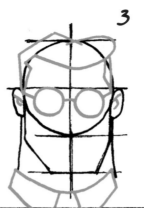 

Step 1: Clark's (or Superman's) head starts with a simple circle. Divide it in half horizontally and vertically. Add another horizontal line half a circle below it. **Step 2:** Clark has a heck of a big jaw that extends down to this horizontal line. His neck is wider than his head. (Most folks don't have such a huge neck, but this is Superman we're drawing!) **Step 3:** Clark's glasses start at the horizontal center line of the circle and extend below it. From this angle, think of the hair as one solid shape. **Step 4:** For the eyes, draw a short curved line with a small black ball in the middle. Place the eyes slightly higher than the center of the glasses. Place the mouth on the horizontal line at the bottom of the circle.

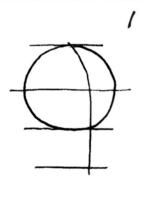 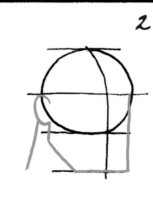  

Step 1: Sketch the circle and jaw line as before. This time, because Clark's head is at a 3/4 angle, the center line curves to the right. **Step 2:** Add the powerful jaw, making sure it's bisected equally by the vertical center line. The neck joins up to the back of the guideline circle. The bottom of the ear begins where the jaw meets the head. **Step 3:** Again, the glasses extend down from the horizontal center line of the circle. Think of the hair as two shapes: an angular shape on the side and a rounded shape on the top. **Step 4:** The nose should be exactly the same length as the ear. (Look in the mirror—it's that way for most people.) The mouth is placed on the horizontal line at the bottom of the circle.

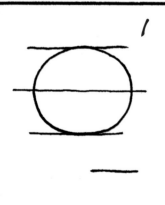 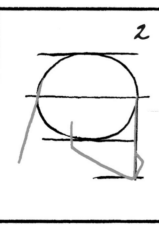  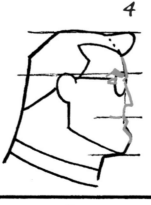

Step 1: For the profile, start with an egg-on-its-side shape, slightly wider than it is tall. **Step 2:** At the back, the neck joins the head at the widest part of the egg shape. At the front, the neck joins far enough forward that it would intersect the eyes if the line continued. Check out that jutting chin and square jaw! **Step 3:** The hair follows the curve of the rounded head, flattening off a little in the back. Notice the little bulge of hair in front, over the forehead. **Step 4:** The mouth, eyes, and nose should all fall in the same proportions that they do from any other angle. The ear and nose are also the same length.

ALL IN PROPORTION

EXPRESSIONS

LIFE IN METROPOLIS CAN BE DRAMATIC! YOU'LL NEED TO SHOW A LOT OF EMOTIONS ON THE FACES OF THESE CHARACTERS.

BUT DON'T WORRY. CHANGING EMOTIONS IS AS EASY AS CHANGING A FEW LINES AROUND THE MOUTH, EYES, AND EYEBROWS.

SAD

FRIGHTENED

SURPRISED

BORED

ANGRY

SNEAKY

STUNNED

TIRED

LAUGHING

HORRIFIED

IN PAIN

ENRAGED

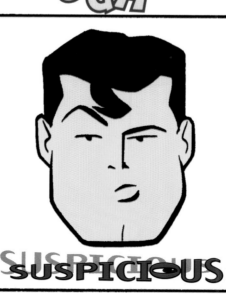

SUSPICIOUS

Study your own face in the mirror, and make some different expressions. As you draw, remember to keep it simple—draw as few lines as possible.

BLUEPRINTS FOR PERFECT HANDS

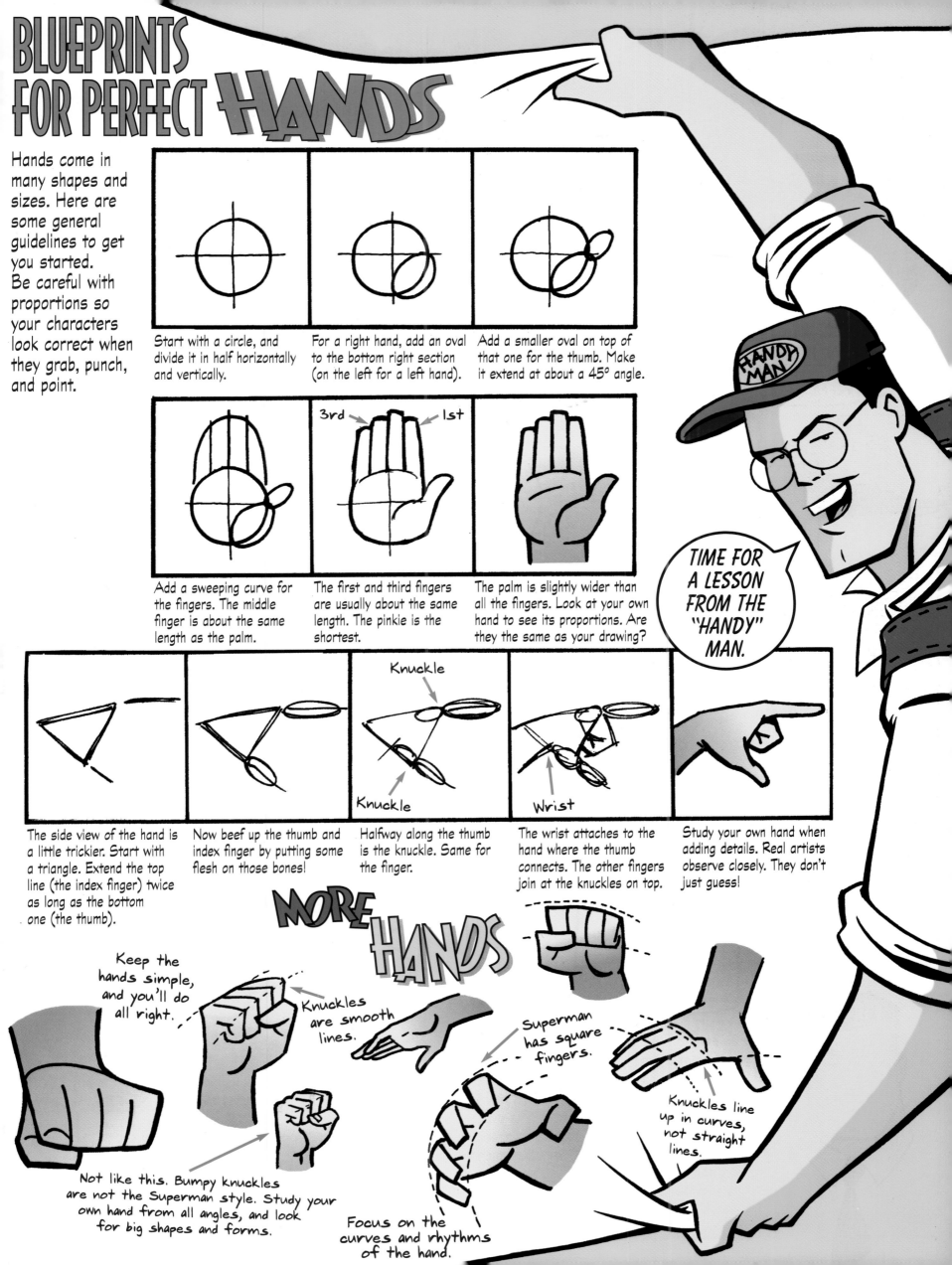

Hands come in many shapes and sizes. Here are some general guidelines to get you started. Be careful with proportions so your characters look correct when they grab, punch, and point.

Start with a circle, and divide it in half horizontally and vertically.

For a right hand, add an oval to the bottom right section (on the left for a left hand).

Add a smaller oval on top of that one for the thumb. Make it extend at about a 45° angle.

Add a sweeping curve for the fingers. The middle finger is about the same length as the palm.

3rd — 1st

The first and third fingers are usually about the same length. The pinkie is the shortest.

The palm is slightly wider than all the fingers. Look at your own hand to see its proportions. Are they the same as your drawing?

TIME FOR A LESSON FROM THE "HANDY" MAN.

The side view of the hand is a little trickier. Start with a triangle. Extend the top line (the index finger) twice as long as the bottom one (the thumb).

Now beef up the thumb and index finger by putting some flesh on those bones!

Knuckle

Knuckle

Halfway along the thumb is the knuckle. Same for the finger.

Wrist

The wrist attaches to the hand where the thumb connects. The other fingers join at the knuckles on top.

Study your own hand when adding details. Real artists observe closely. They don't just guess!

MORE HANDS

Keep the hands simple, and you'll do all right.

Knuckles are smooth lines.

Superman has square fingers.

Knuckles line up in curves, not straight lines.

Not like this. Bumpy knuckles are not the Superman style. Study your own hand from all angles, and look for big shapes and forms.

Focus on the curves and rhythms of the hand.

Foreshortening the figure isn't hard, but now it's going to be even easier. First, draw that skeleton figure you already learned, but add circles to the elbows and wrists. This will help you make the parts bigger or smaller as you foreshorten the arms.

Look closely at the drawing to the left. Can you see how, as the arm bends and moves toward you, the hand gets much bigger and the lines on the sides of the arm become shorter? The same system works for foreshortening legs, fingers, or whole bodies. Lightly sketch the skeleton figure, and see if you've made the parts big or small in a way that makes the arms look like they're coming toward you.

CLARK'S TIPS

The smaller shape should never be drawn in front. Shapes always get bigger as they come toward you. No exceptions.

This isn't a tube, it's a section of a cone.

This isn't a box, it's a cowbell. **MOOOO!**

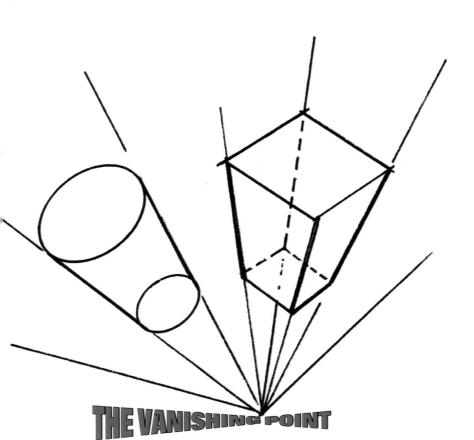

THE VANISHING POINT

A LITTLE BIT ABOUT SOMETHING CALLED THE
VANISHING POINT

As Superman throws this nasty bit of radioactive metal away, notice that it becomes not just a bit smaller but a LOT smaller. In fact, because of his super strength, Superman can throw it so far away that it will eventually disappear from sight at a place called the **vanishing point.** In a drawing, all things get smaller as they move in space toward the vanishing point. You'll find out more about this mysterious place later in this book.

ARE YOU READY FOR YOUR FIRST SUPER DRAWING?

UP, UP, AND AWAY!

Start by sketching the most important parts of the gesture drawing: the spine, ribs, hips, and head (in that order).

Notice the extreme foreshortening of the arms and hands on this figure. He's flying right out at you, so make the hands large.

Once the gesture drawing is correct, it's time to **flesh out** the rest of the character. Put some meat on those bones!

Remember the lesson on hands? This is a terrific place where it comes in... ahem...handy.

Draw lightly so any mistakes can be easily corrected. When you're happy with your sketch, ink over it in black, and then erase the pencil lines.

Now bring out the markers and colored pencils to finish the drawing!

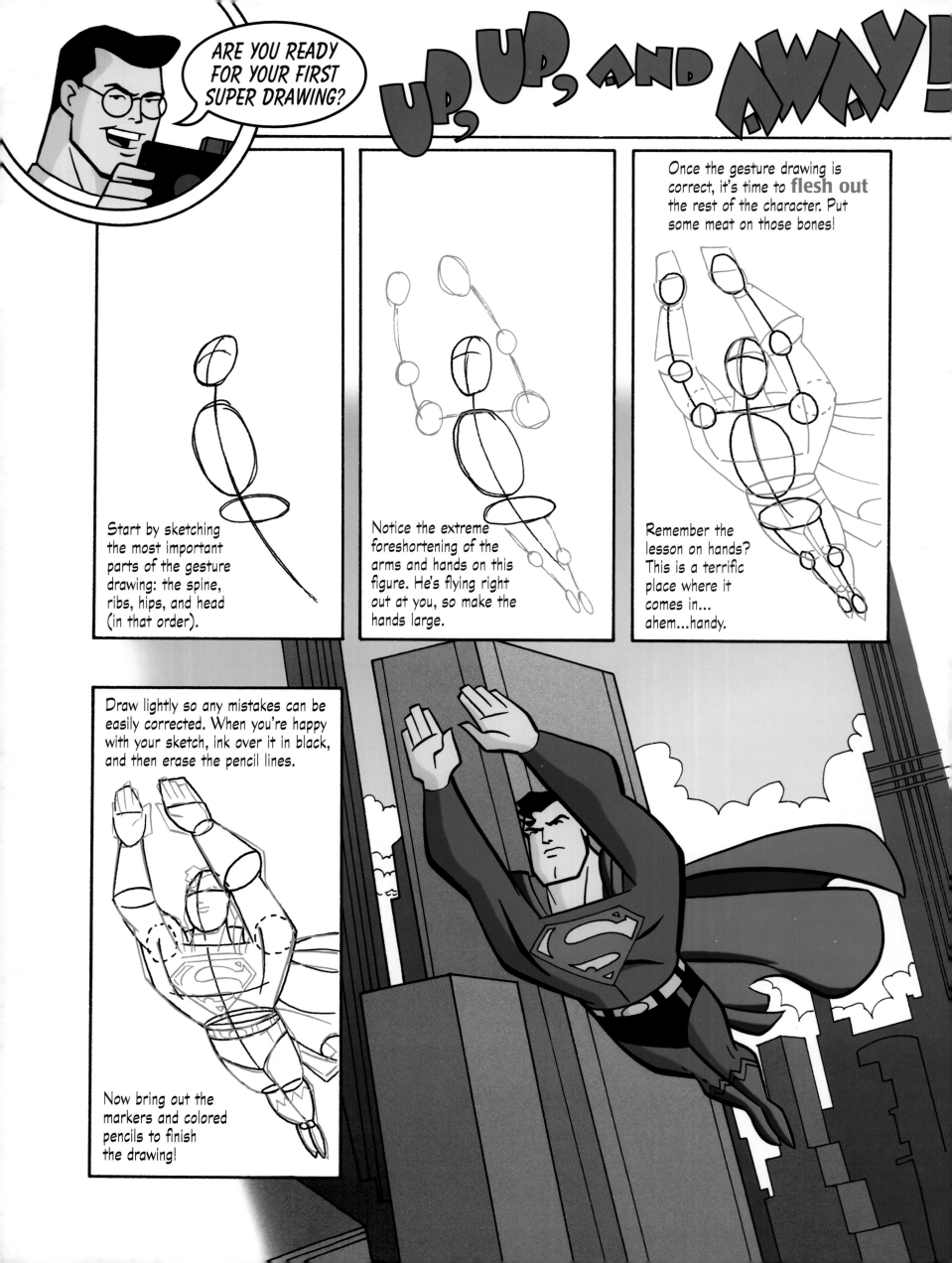

WHILE PATROLLING ABOVE THE CITY, THE MAN OF STEEL LISTENS FOR EMERGENCIES THOUSANDS OF FEET BELOW HIM WITH HIS SUPER HEARING.

This drawing shows how flexible the spine can be. You can see quite a bend in his backbone here.

Superman is leaning forward, so his head is in front of part of his body. When something like this happens, you should still draw the parts you won't be able to see so everything will be in correct proportion later. This is called **drawing through**—good artists always do it.

Notice Superman's left leg. The inside of the leg is a relatively straight line, while the outside is drawn with curves.

This relationship between curved and straight lines is very much the Superman style of drawing figures.

Straight

Curved

When you have everything in proportion, it's time to ink over the lines with a marker and color it in.

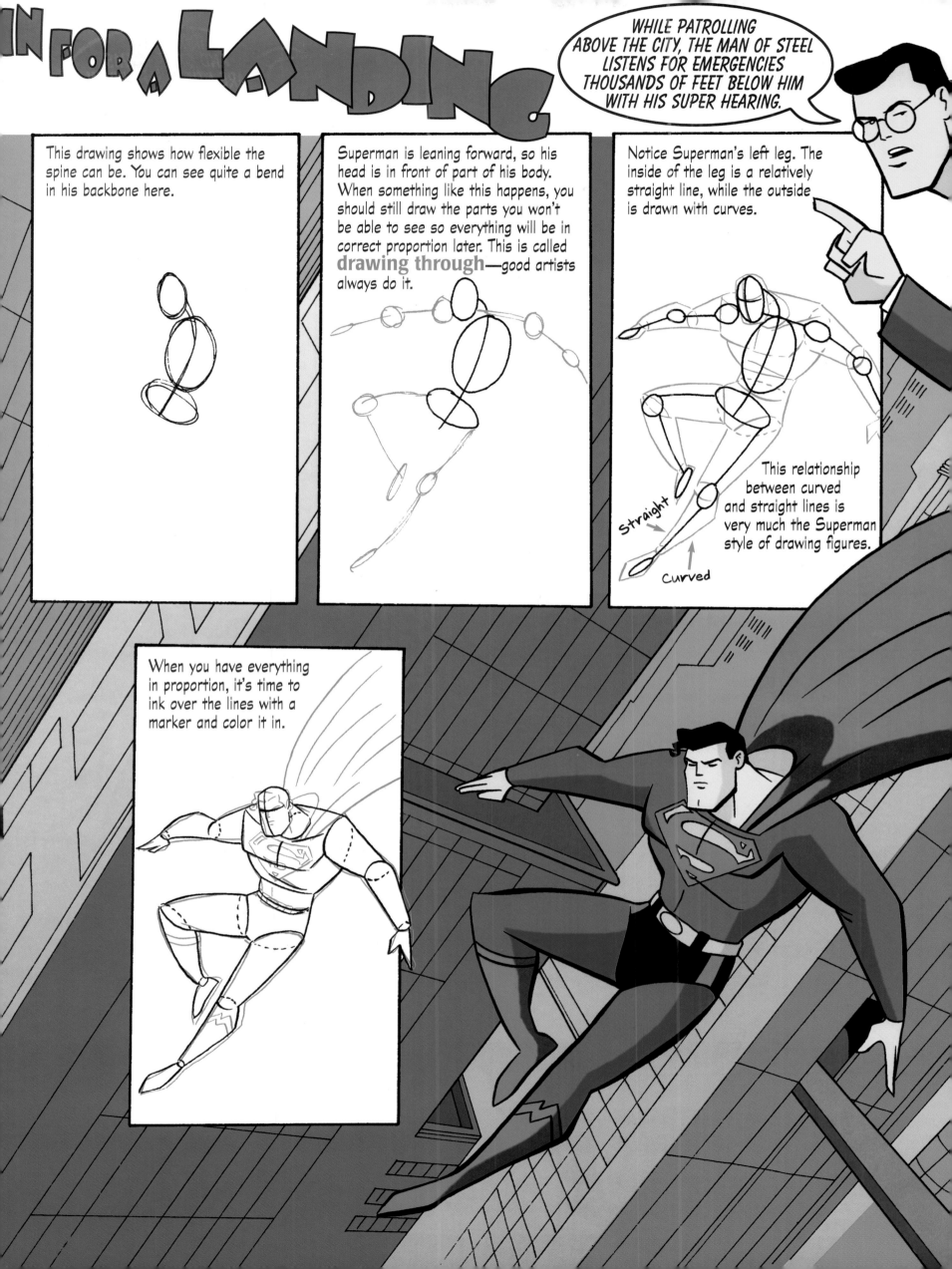

Bends Steel in His Bare Hands

IRON BARS AND STEEL BEAMS ARE NEVER SAFE WHEN SUPERMAN'S AROUND.

As always, begin by drawing the spine, ribs, hips, and head.

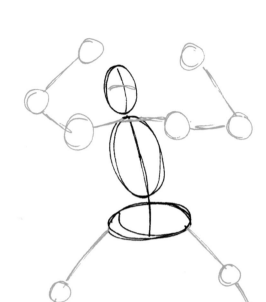

Careful with the foreshortening of Superman's arms on this one.

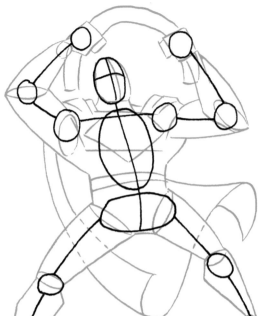

His hands are the closest thing to you—that's why they're so much bigger than his head!

Time to ink over the pencil lines and color your drawing.

The Man of STEEL

DAILY PLANET ™

Superman Saves the Day!

You know the routine—spine, ribs, hips, and head! But this drawing helps show a little about balance in the figure. All the incredible weight that Superman is holding up has to be balanced or he'd fall over.

A man's **center of gravity** is around his shoulders. Look at the final drawing and notice that Superman's arms and legs are balanced on either side of his center of gravity to keep the figure looking steady.

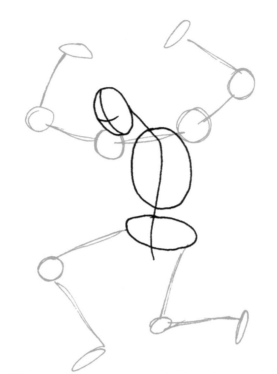

When adding arms and feet, keep that center of gravity.

Balancing your figure is important for any drawing...

...not just one where Superman is lifting up a heavy weight.

Careful with that chest emblem! Observe the shapes closely when copying the S.

Time to ink and color!

TIME TO TALK ABOUT SUPERMAN'S AMAZING...

HEAT VISION

I'VE GOT TO REMEMBER TO TAKE OFF MY GLASSES FIRST!

CLARK'S HOT TIPS

When you draw the heat vision, the straighter the lines, the better the drawing. So use your straightedge for the heat vision effect.

Even though this isn't a full-figure illustration, you still start with the spine and ribs. The head goes on last.

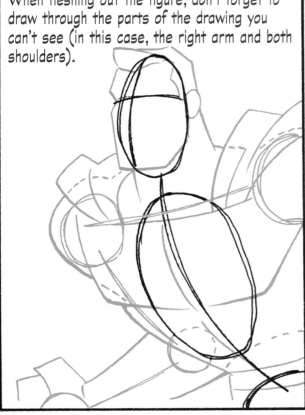

When fleshing out the figure, don't forget to draw through the parts of the drawing you can't see (in this case, the right arm and both shoulders).

Drawing through allows you to draw the cape properly and helps you put the forearm in the correct place.

Now it's time to ink and color, just like the finished drawing below.

POWERS!

The strong thrust of the backbone often continues down into one (or a few) of the limbs. In this case, Superman's left leg stretches out in the same direction as his spine, exaggerating the movement of the pose. This idea is often referred to as the **line of action** in a gesture.

ONE OF SUPERMAN'S GREATEST POWERS IS THAT HE IS...

Once again, you can see the amazing flexibility of the spine. This time, it's thrust forward so that Superman's chest can take the brunt of Luthor's death ray.

Try to keep the strong line of action when fleshing out the forms.

...INVULNERABLE

Did you notice the straight and curved lines in Superman's arms and legs in this pose? Of course you did!

With Superman, try to make every gesture large and exaggerated. He is super, after all!

The S shield is easy if you make sure the yellow and red shapes are drawn correctly.

Look at the yellow and red areas as shapes you have to copy.

CLARK'S TIPS

Can you see the line of action in all of these poses? Try to find it in the other poses in this book too.

The Female

Three Basic Differences in Structure

1 You probably know the first one. Men tend to be larger, taller, heavier, and broader than women (see the skeletons to the right). Although huge women and little men exist, most people tend to be the other way around.

2 The second is less obvious. A man has a wide upper section (shoulders and ribs) and small hips. A woman usually has wide hips and a small upper body. This difference causes a woman's center of gravity to be in her hips, while a man's center of gravity is in his upper body (top of the ribs, near the neck).

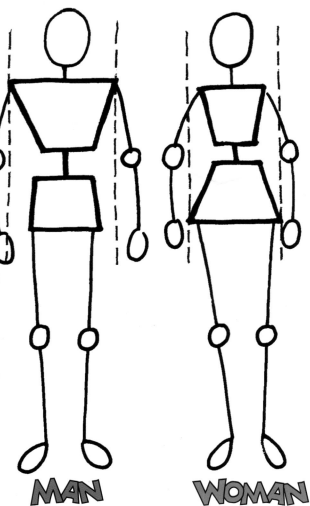

MAN WOMAN

WOMAN MAN

3 A woman's hips have a strong tilt that can easily be seen when she stands sideways. To make up for this hip tilt, her upper body tilts back the other way, giving a woman's upright posture a lot of curve. On the other hand, a man's pelvis tilts only slightly, giving him a more rigid posture when standing straight.

On average a woman's body may be shorter than a man's, but she is still eight heads tall!

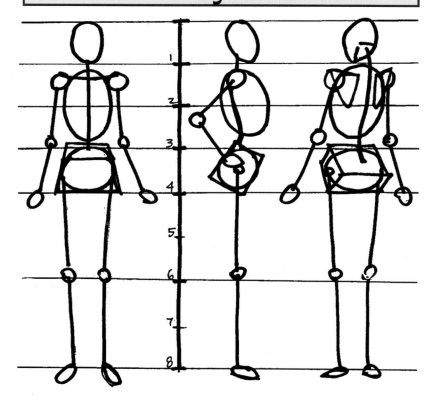

IT STILL WORKS BECAUSE MY HEAD IS JUST A TEENY BIT LARGER THAN THAT OF THE WOMAN TO MY RIGHT.

Form

Female Features

WOMEN AND MEN COME IN EVERY POSSIBLE SHAPE AND SIZE. IT'S EASY TO LEARN SOME BASIC TYPES AND GENERAL RULES.

Brow and bridge of the nose have gentler curves than a man's.

Nose is smaller and pointier.

Lois Lane

Neck is smaller and thinner.

Cheeks are soft, continuous curves, usually leading to a small, pointed chin.

LANA LANG

Lips are fuller and usually colored red or pink.

Martha (Ma) Kent

Eyebrows are thin, simple shapes.

Eyelashes are much thicker and are drawn as one shape, not a lot of little lash lines.

MAGGIE SAWYER

THE HANDS

Fingers are thin and tapered.

Knuckles are always curved lines.

Objects look bigger in small female hands.

These hands are obviously female. Can you tell what makes them different from a man's hand?

Wrist is smaller than palm.

MY BEST FRIEND IS ALSO MY CLOSEST RIVAL. THE DAILY PLANET HAS TWO ACE REPORTERS AND THE OTHER ONE IS...

Lois

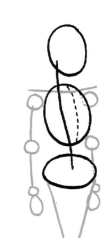

Lois is wearing loose-fitting clothes, but the steps for drawing her don't change in the slightest. You still start with the same four shapes: spine, ribs, hips, and head. Don't forget the feminine curve in her spine.

Even though Lois is standing straight, notice the subtle curves in her stance. That's the natural way people stand, with a sort of rhythm to their posture.

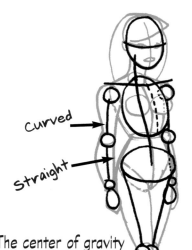

Curved

Straight

The center of gravity in this pose is over her hips—can you tell? Her head and feet seem to extend from her hips. Also notice the straight and curved lines of her right arm.

The clothes are easy to draw. Just keep gravity in mind when drawing her skirt. It falls directly down from the hips and fans out from there. Now you're ready to ink and color.

Lane

Lois is leaning way out, putting all her weight on her right leg. This sort of pose is easy to draw if you think about her center of gravity!

If you draw a line directly down from her head, you'll find it goes through her forward leg. This leg is carrying all her weight, and her trailing leg is for balance.

Look at that left leg. There's that old straight and curved relationship happening again!

Think of her clothes as large, basic shapes.

The skirt and jacket cover her form rather closely, and they stretch as she moves her leg. When you think you have it, you're ready to ink and color.

SUPERMAN IS A MAN OF TWO WORLDS—EARTH AND KRYPTON. THAT ALSO MAKES HIM A MAN WITH TWO SETS OF PARENTS. EVEN FOR SUPERMAN, IT'S NICE TO HAVE...

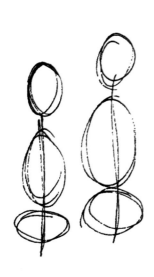

This portrait of Martha and Jonathan Kent gives you an opportunity to examine the differences between men and women in one drawing! Right off the bat, you can see who is taller!

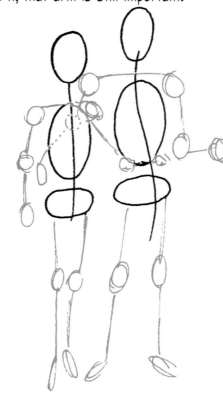

Remember to **draw through** for Jonathan's arm. Even though you can't see it, that arm is still important.

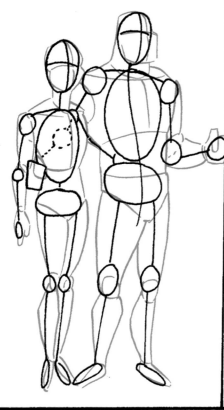

Add some shapes to the forms. Who is bigger? Bulkier?

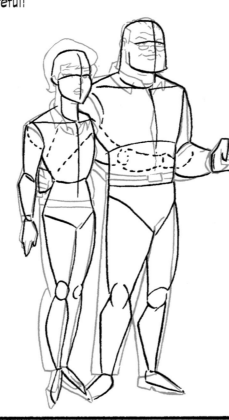

Lots of straight and curved lines here. Careful!

...Family

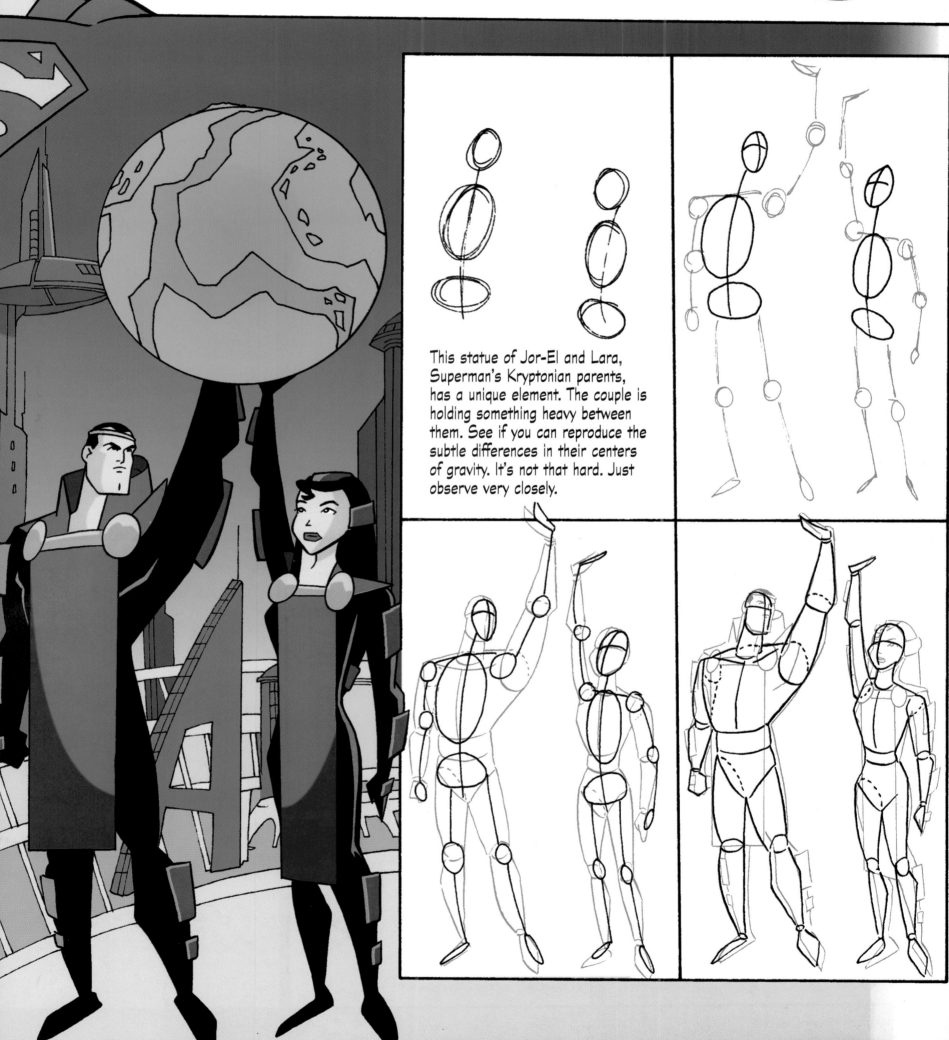

This statue of Jor-El and Lara, Superman's Kryptonian parents, has a unique element. The couple is holding something heavy between them. See if you can reproduce the subtle differences in their centers of gravity. It's not that hard. Just observe very closely.

Star Reporter for the

DAILY PLANET ™

Get the basic skeleton right, and it's easy to draw the finished figure.

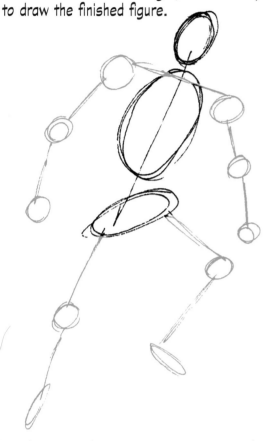

Trying to guess where arms and shoulders should be inside loose clothing would be murder...

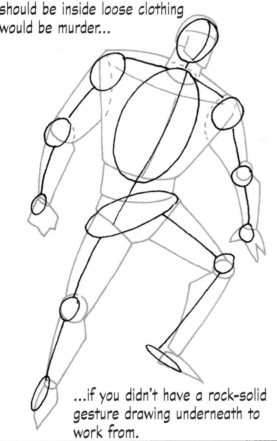

...if you didn't have a rock-solid gesture drawing underneath to work from.

When your rock-solid drawing is done, you can ink and color it in.

Add some super color to this classic pose!

THIS LOOKS LIKE A JOB FOR...SUPERMAN!

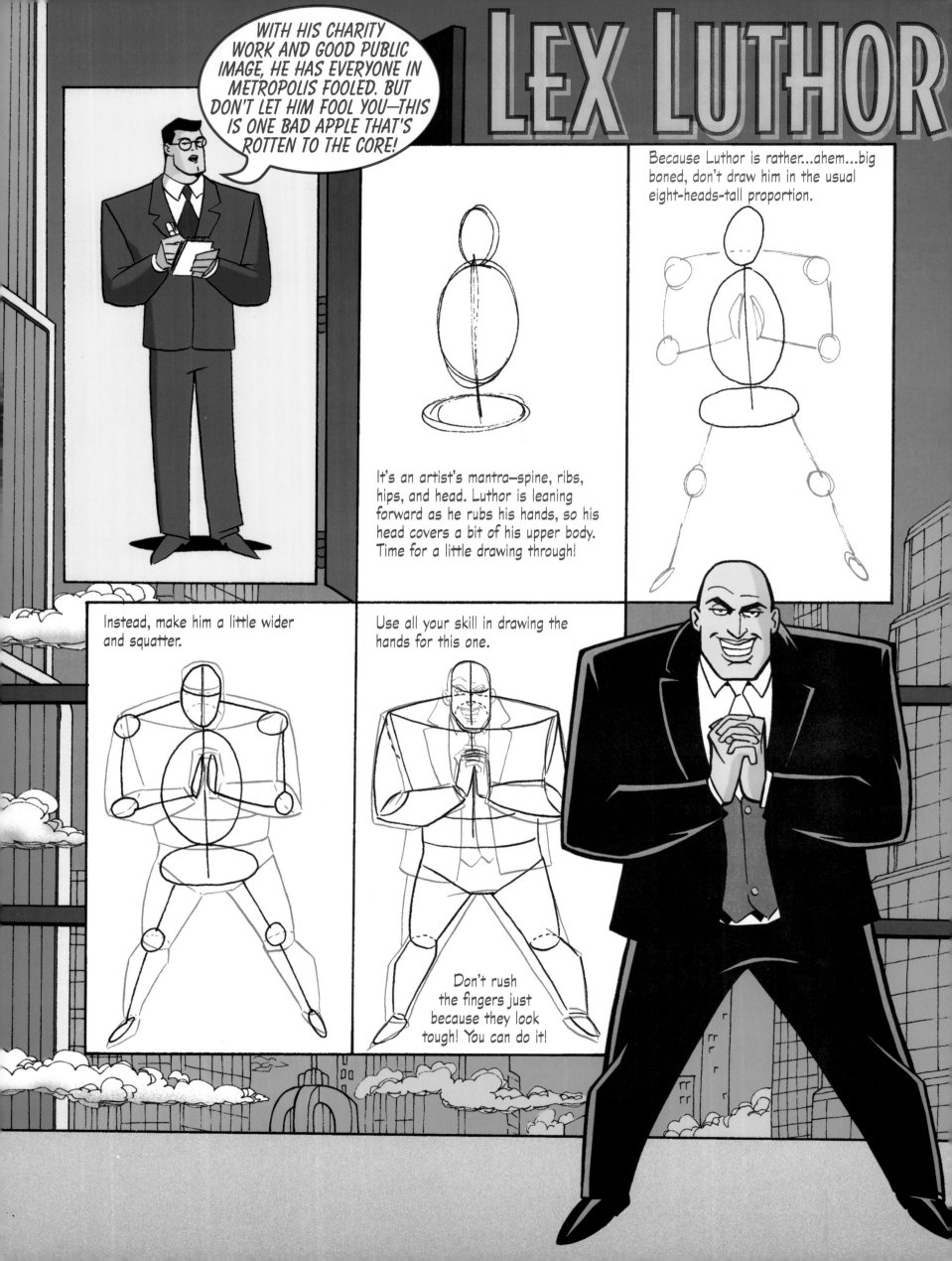

PARASITE

HAVING ALL THE SUPERPOWERS IN THE WORLD DOESN'T DO MUCH GOOD AGAINST A CREATURE WHO CAN SUCK THE POWER RIGHT OUT OF YOU...AND INTO HIMSELF!

This pose is a little off balance, which gives it a sense of movement and action! Can you see the line of action in the drawing?

One arm is up in the air, and the other is down. One leg is extended, while the other is close to the body. This kind of posing is called **Asymmetry**.

Asymmetry makes your drawing more lifelike.

Despite the fact that the Parasite has a weird, pointy head, you start this pose the same as always. By now, that should be second nature to you!

Ready to ink and color in this evil villain? Better hurry up before he siphons your drawing ability!

Mr. Mxyzptlk

THIS MAGICAL IMP FROM THE FIFTH DIMENSION IS NOTHING BUT TROUBLE!

Mr. Mxyzptlk is a tricky one to draw! His figure is way off the standard eight heads high, but you still construct him the usual way—starting with spine, ribs, hips, and head.

Only the sizes of his head, arms, and legs are different.

His skeleton fits together like a regular human's does—it's just in different proportions.

Since his proportions are so different, you have to be extra careful with them.

Don't make his body too short or his head too big.

When the proportions look correct (or properly incorrect, really)...

...it's time to ink, erase, and color. For this drawing, be sure to use **magic** markers!

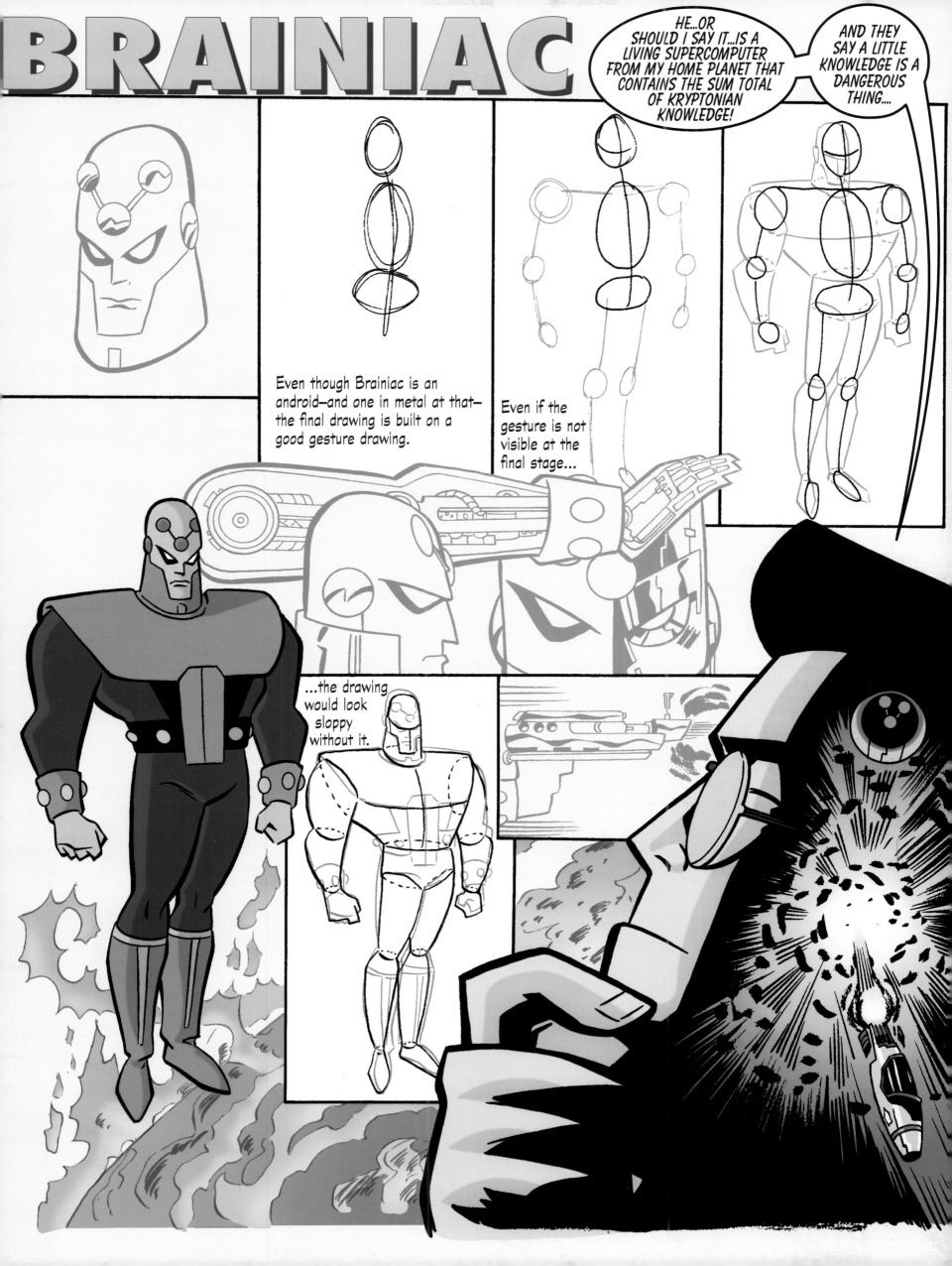

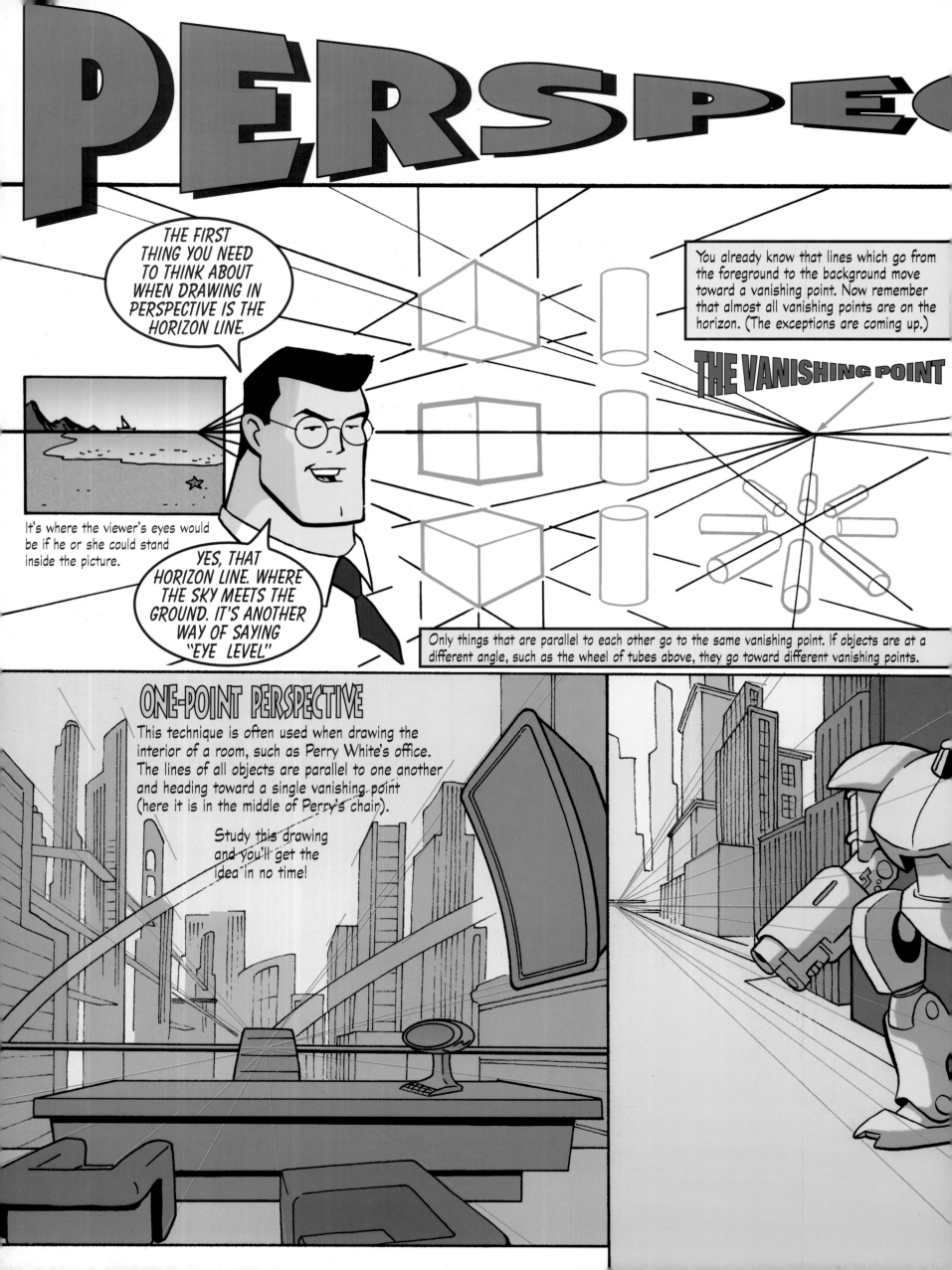

PERSPE(

THE FIRST THING YOU NEED TO THINK ABOUT WHEN DRAWING IN PERSPECTIVE IS THE HORIZON LINE.

It's where the viewer's eyes would be if he or she could stand inside the picture.

YES, THAT HORIZON LINE. WHERE THE SKY MEETS THE GROUND. IT'S ANOTHER WAY OF SAYING "EYE LEVEL."

You already know that lines which go from the foreground to the background move toward a vanishing point. Now remember that almost all vanishing points are on the horizon. (The exceptions are coming up.)

THE VANISHING POINT

Only things that are parallel to each other go to the same vanishing point. If objects are at a different angle, such as the wheel of tubes above, they go toward different vanishing points.

ONE-POINT PERSPECTIVE

This technique is often used when drawing the interior of a room, such as Perry White's office. The lines of all objects are parallel to one another and heading toward a single vanishing point (here it is in the middle of Perry's chair).

Study this drawing and you'll get the idea in no time!

Perspective is the representation of objects in three-dimensional space to give the illusion of depth and distance. *(WHEW!)*

CIRCLES IN PERSPECTIVE

You can even draw circles in perspective. Watch, it's quite easy. First, see how a circle fits inside a square?

If you put the square in perspective by moving the parallel lines to a vanishing point, it changes the shape of the square. Fit the circle inside the square again, and the shape becomes an oval. That's all there is to drawing a circle in perspective.

As long as the square is in proper perspective, the circle inside it will be as well!

THREE-POINT PERSPECTIVE

You learned that **almost** all vanishing points are on the horizon? Here are the exceptions. When you wish to show how incredibly tall something is (like the skyscrapers of Metropolis), you may put a third vanishing point in the sky. The other two vanishing points stay on the horizon where they belong! If you want to show how very far down something is (for instance, while looking down from the top of a tall building), you might put a third vanishing point deep in the ground. It's all up to you!

TWO-POINT PERSPECTIVE

This technique is used when the viewer is looking at a scene from an angle. A corner of each building is closest to the viewer. The sides of each building recede to one of two vanishing points on the horizon line. Remember, all the vertical lines are parallel to the frame of the drawing.

PUTTING THE FIGURE IN

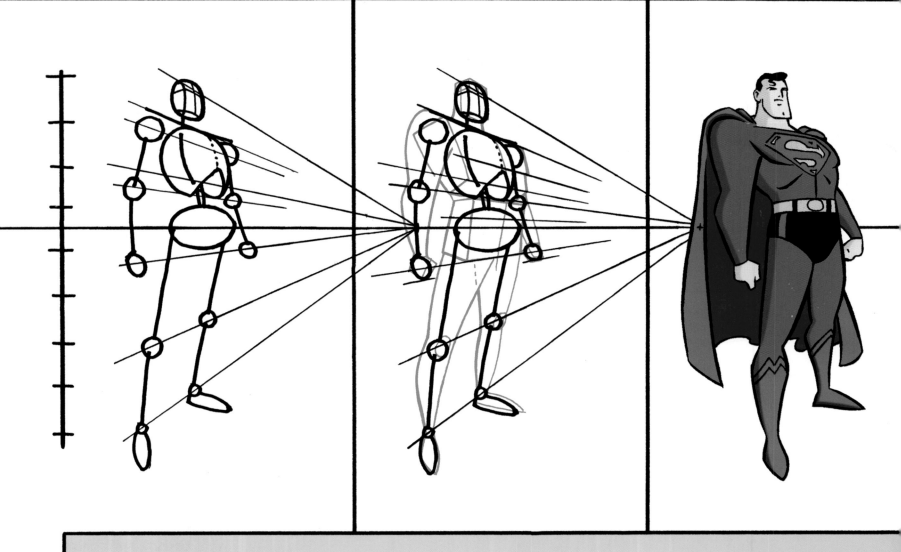

Buildings and cars aren't the only things that follow the rules of perspective. Everything does. Even people! The trouble is that it's hard to visualize the perspective clearly with all those rounded shapes.

Just make sure all the ankles, knees, shoulders, and wrists are parallel and can be drawn to the same vanishing point. It helps to picture the head, torso, and hips as boxes for this exercise.

Ta-Dah! Using a vanishing point makes foreshortening a lot easier, don' you think? You don't have to guess where the parts go.

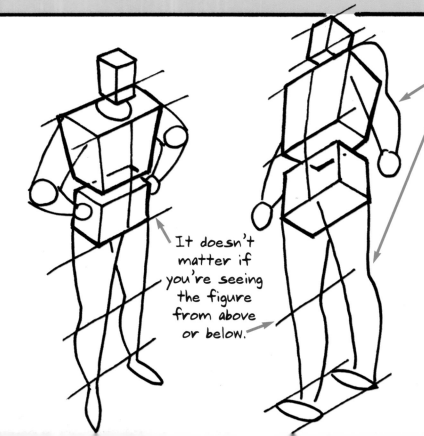

It doesn't matter if you're seeing the figure from above or below.

Notice all of the parts that line up-shoulders, hips, knees, and ankles.

CLARK'S TIPS

Boxes help with foreshortening, but they're not good for establishing your line of action on a stick-figure skeleton. So don't use boxes to create action and gesture poses.

PERSPECTIVE

Next Question:

How do you put more than one figure in a drawing? Perspective says closer figures appear larger, and figures farther away appear smaller. But how small? How big?

Some artists use a complicated set of rules for perspective, but here's an easy shortcut. Place the horizon line through the same part of each figure. Notice above, it's through each person's ankle.

Here, the horizon line is through the figures' hips. Just make sure they're positioned on the line in the same place.

These figures are below the horizon. To get the perspective right, first draw Superman the size you wish. Then count how many heads down he is from the horizon line. Count the same number of head lengths for Lex Luthor and Lois Lane. (Use the same size head that you're drawing on the figures.) See? It's no problem!

If you think of the body parts as boxes, it's easier to put them in perspective. You'll be able to do it from any angle.

BET YOU NEVER KNEW DRAWING WAS GOING TO BE THIS EASY!

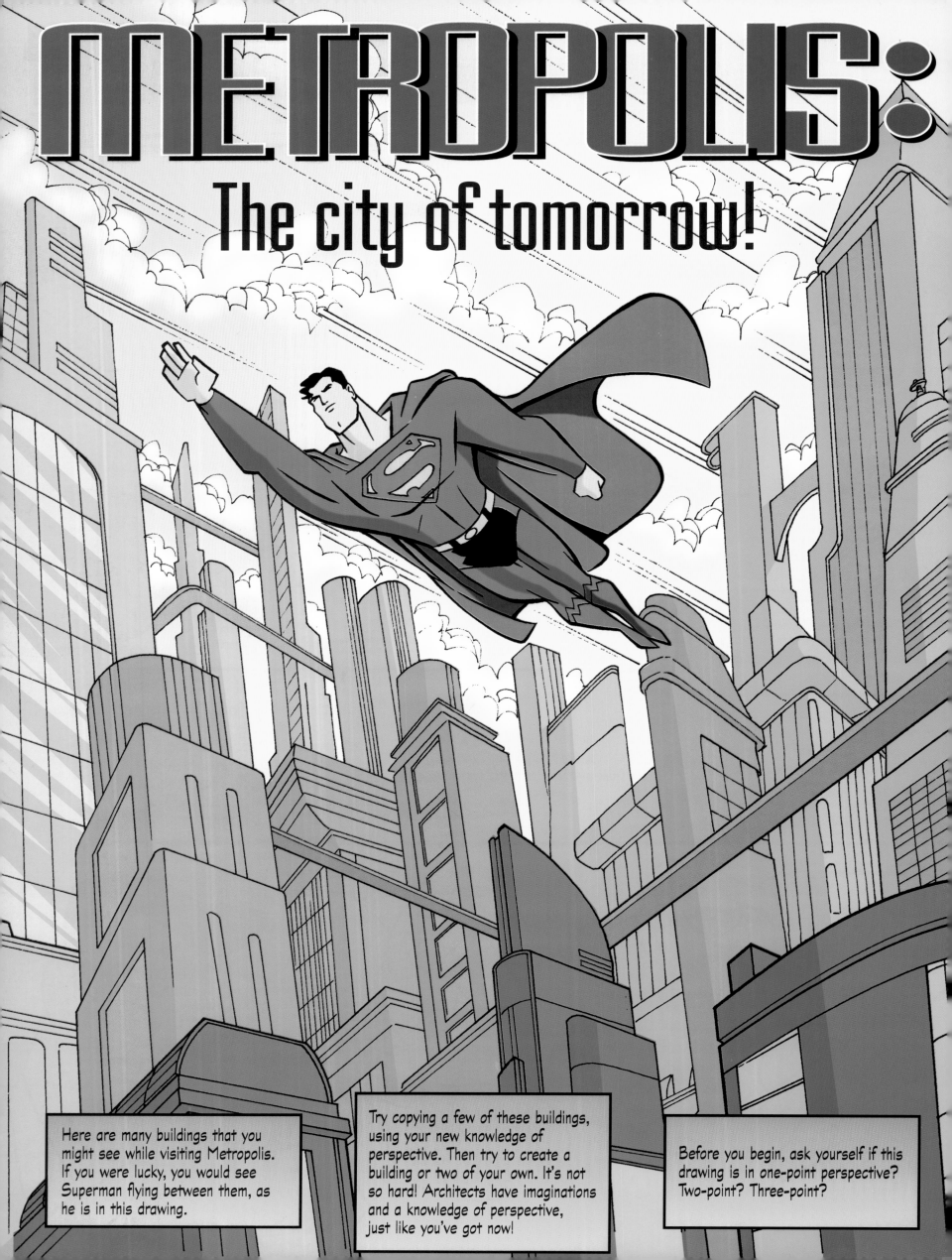

METROPOLIS:
The city of tomorrow!

Here are many buildings that you might see while visiting Metropolis. If you were lucky, you would see Superman flying between them, as he is in this drawing.

Try copying a few of these buildings, using your new knowledge of perspective. Then try to create a building or two of your own. It's not so hard! Architects have imaginations and a knowledge of perspective, just like you've got now!

Before you begin, ask yourself if this drawing is in one-point perspective? Two-point? Three-point?